It's A Wonderful Life

Special thanks to
Patty Rice for her support.

It's a Wonderful Life

ISBN: 0-7407-3841-0

Library of Congress Control Number: 2003102244

04 05 06 07 KFO 10 9 8 7 6 5 4 3 2

PHOTO CREDITS

The Frank Capra Archives at Wesleyan University, the Academy of Motion Picture Arts and Sciences, the UCLA Theatre Arts Library, the Donna Reed Foundation, and Bud Barnett at Cinema Collectors.

IT'S A Wonderful Life

Favorite Scenes from the Classic Film

JIMMY HAWKINS

**Andrews McMeel
Publishing**

Kansas City

$\mathcal{I}$t's a Wonderful Life brings back so many wonderful memories. I played the youngest member of the cast, Tommy Bailey. Since then I've worked with or stayed in touch with those associated with the making of what has become the most beloved movie of our time. Through reminiscing with Frank Capra, Jimmy Stewart, Donna Reed, and other cast and crew members I feel we've been able to capture in pictures and dialogue the favorite moments of all of us who were there . . . and to share with you our wonderful memories of *It's a Wonderful Life.*

Jimmy Hawkins

GOWER

J owe everything to George Bailey
Help him, dear lord.

MARY

J love him, dear lord.
Watch over him tonight.

ZUZU

*P*lease bring Daddy home.

ANGEL'S VOICE

George Bailey . . . yes, tonight's his crucial night. He'll be thinking of throwing away God's greatest gift. Joseph, send for Clarence.

CLARENCE

Sir, if I accomplish my mission, might I perhaps win my wings?

I'm going out exploring someday,
you watch.

*G*eorge Bailey, I'll love you till
the day I die.

Mr. Gower, you don't know what you're doing. You got that telegram and you're upset. Look at the bottle you took the powder from. It's poison.

$\mathcal{B}$IG—see! I don't want one
for one night. I want something
for a thousand nights. A great big one.

Harry and I have it all figured out. Harry will take my job at the Building and Loan, work there for four years, then he'll go. I couldn't face being cooped up in a shabby little office. I want to do something big, something important.

MARY

You pass me on the street every day.

GEORGE

That was a little girl
named Mary Hatch. That wasn't you.

*B*uffalo gals can't you come out
tonight? And dance by the light
of the moon.

*M*ary, I know what I'm going to do
tomorrow and the next day and the next
year and the year after that. I'm shaking
the dust of this crummy little town off
my feet and I'm going to see the world.

GEORGE

What did you wish for when you threw the rock at the old Granville House? You want the moon? Just say the word and I'll throw a lasso around it and pull it down.

This town needs this measly one-horse institution if only to have someplace where people can come without crawling to Potter.

George got four years older
waiting for Harry to
come back from college and
take over the Building and Loan.

GEORGE

What's a pretty girl like you
doing marrying this
two-headed brother of mine?

RUTH

It's purely mercenary.
My father offered him a job.

MRS. BAILEY

Looks like she can keep
Harry on his toes.

GEORGE

Keep him out of
Bedford Falls, anyway.

MRS. BAILEY

Did you know Mary Hatch
is back from school?

GEORGE

I thought you'd go back to New York like Sam and the rest of them.

MARY

I guess I was homesick.

GEORGE

Homesick? For Bedford Falls?

Now listen to me! I don't want any plastics. I don't want any ground floors, and I don't want to get married.

MRS. BAILEY

First Harry, now George.
Annie, we're just two old maids now.

ANNIE

You speak for yourself, Mrs. B.

Don't look now but there's something funny going on over at the bank, George. I've never really seen one, but that's got all the earmarks of a run.

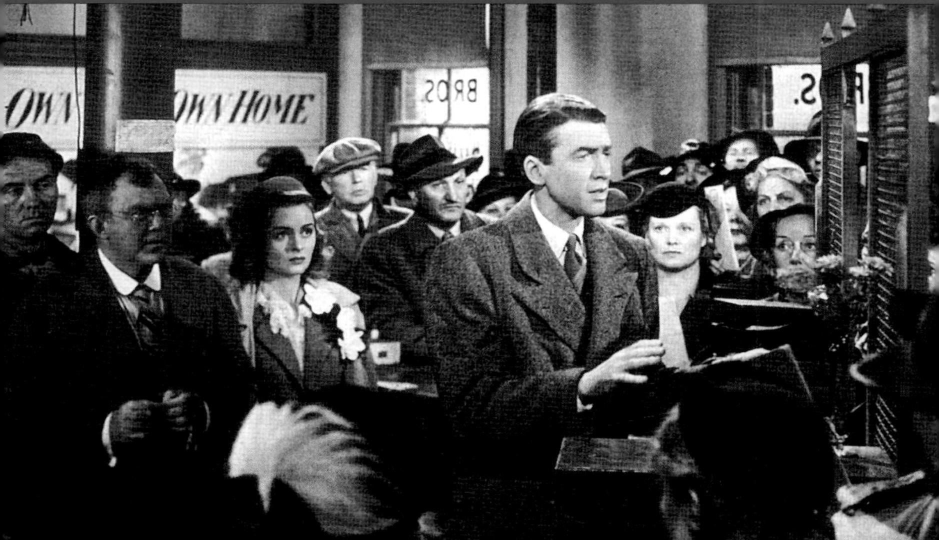
OWN HOME

The money's not here. Your money's in Joe's house and in the Kennedys' house. You're lending them the money to build. What are you going to do? Foreclose on them? I have two thousand dollars that will tide us over until the bank reopens.

GEORGE

Oh, Mary . . .

MARY

Remember the night we broke
the windows in this old house?
This is what I wished for.

GEORGE

Darling, you're wonderful.

MARY

*B*read! That this house may never know hunger. Salt! That life may always have flavor.

GEORGE

*A*nd wine! That joy and prosperity may reign forever. Enter the Martini castle.

*N*o . . . no . . . no, now wait a minute.
The answer is no. No! Doggone it! I won't
work for you at any price. You sit around
here and spin your little web and think
the whole world revolves around you and
your money. Well, it doesn't, Mr. Potter!
In the . . . in the whole vast configuration
of things, I'd say you were nothing but a
scurvy little spider. You . . .

I didn't want to marry anybody else
in town. I want my baby to look like you.
George Bailey lassos the stork.

Mary, Janie, and Pete

Fixing up the Granville house

Helping out at the USO

Mr. Gower raising war bonds

*N*ow, you probably already guessed that George never leaves Bedford Falls. Mary had her baby, a boy. Then a girl. She worked to make the Granville house a home. Then came the war. Mary had two more babies but found time to run the USO. Potter headed up the draft board. Gower and Uncle Billy sold war bonds.

George was four-F but fought the fight of Bedford Falls. He was made air raid warden. Bert got the Silver Star. Ernie parachuted into France. Everyone wept and prayed on V-E day and V-J day. Harry topped them all—shot down fifteen planes and was awarded the Congressional Medal of Honor. Bedford Falls celebrated.

Harry Bailey

George

Bert the cop

KILROY WAS HERE

AFTER 5 DAYS RETURN TO

Sgt. Bert Bond 39749472
27th Infantry
APO #832 Postmaster

PASSED BY
U 00054 S
ARMY EXAMINER

VIA AIR MAIL

George & Mary Bailey
320 Sycamore
Bedford Falls
New York

Carter . . . bank examiner.
He wants accounts payable.

Where's the money, you stupid, silly old fool? Where's the money? Do you realize what this means? It means bankruptcy and scandal and prison. That's what it means. One of us is going to jail. Well, it's not going to be me.

MARY

Hello, Darling.

PETE

How do you spell frankincense?

JANIE

I've been practicing.

TOMMY

S'cuse me, s'cuse me.

Isn't that wonderful about Harry? We're
famous, George. I bet I had
fifty calls about the parade, the banquet.
Better hurry and shave. The families will
be here soon.

Families, I don't want the families
over here.

ZUZU

Look Daddy . . . paste it.

GEORGE

Yeah, all right. Now I'll
paste this together.
There it is, good as new.

PETE

Daddy, how do you spell "Hallelujah"?

GEORGE

How should I know? What do
you think I am, a dictionary? Tommy,
stop that! Stop it! Janie, Janie, haven't
you learned that silly tune yet!
You've played it over and over again.
Now stop it! Stop it!

*L*ook at you. You use to be so cocky! You were going to go out and conquer the world. You once called me a warped, frustrated old man. What are you but a warped, frustrated young man? A miserable little clerk crawling in here on your hands and knees and begging for help. No securities—no stocks—no bonds— nothing but a miserable little five hundred dollar equity in a life insurance policy. You're worth more dead than alive.

God . . . God . . . Dear Father in Heaven.
I'm not a praying man, but if
you're up there and can hear me,
show me the way. I'm at the end of
my rope. Show me the way, God.

Help! Help! Help!

CLARENCE

I'm your guardian angel, the answer to your prayer.

GEORGE

What happened to your wings?

CLARENCE

I haven't earned them yet.

GEORGE

I wish I'd never been born.

CLARENCE

Oh, you mustn't say things like that. Wait a minute, that's an idea. You've got your wish. You've never been born.

Hey . . . hey. Where did the Building and Loan move to?

CLARENCE

You've been given a great gift, George!
A chance to see what the world
would be like without you.

GEORGE

Mother, this is George. I thought sure
you would remember me.

MA BAILEY

George who? If you're looking for a room
there's no vacancy.

Strange, isn't it? Each man's life touches so many other lives, and when he isn't around it leaves an awful hole, doesn't he? You see, George, you really had a wonderful life. Don't you see what a mistake it would be to throw it away?

Mary, it's George! Don't you know me? What happened to us?

I don't know you! Let me go!

Mary, please! Oh, don't do this to me. Please, Mary, help me. Where's our kids? I need you, Mary! Help me, Mary!

Clarence! Clarence! Help me, Clarence.
Get me back. Get me back.
I don't care what happens to me.
Only get me back to my wife and kids.
Help me, Clarence, please. Please!
I want to live again!

Hello, Bedford Falls!

GEORGE

Mary! Kids! Janie—Tommy!
ZuZu, my little gingersnap!

MARY

George, darling!

A toast . . . to my big brother, George.
The richest man in town.

ZUZU

*L*ook, daddy. Teacher says every time a bell rings an angel gets his wings.

GEORGE

*T*hat's right. Attaboy, Clarence.

A Wonderful Cast

Auld Lang Syne